Serendipity Stories of Cats and Their People

BY ESTHER G. JOHNSON

Illustrated by Phyllis Lahti

Enjoy!

Esther G. Johnson

Table of Contents

Acknowledgments   v

Introduction   vii

Dedication   ix

Chapter:

1. Theodore, Ginger and Skyehill living.   3

2. Cat Fact and Fancy.   17

3. Buffalo Bill Lives.   31

4. Regal Reggie.   41

5. And More Library Cats.   51

6 A Second Hand Bookstore with Heart.   69

7. Madam Meadow's Cat House.   83

8. Guardians of Treasure.   95

9. When the Cat Got My Tongue.   109

Acknowledgement

Sincere thanks to all who shared their stories and generously gave permission to weave them into the narrative of my book: Mibs and Walter Swanson, Marjorie Caygill of the British Museum, Phyllis Lahti, Yvonne Saddler, Jan Louch, Verle Parker, Vicki Myron, Shelley K., Ann Christensen, Alice Meadow, Sigrid Skaaland, Margaret and Ruth Carlson, and Ruth Harper McKee.

A special thanks to my sister, Dagny, who gave the support I needed in order to keep writing and who spent many hours locating for eradication all those gremlins that disrupted the smooth flow of the stories.

Introduction

Horace Walpole, who lived from 1717 to 1797, coined the word "serendipity" after reading a fairy tale called "Three Princes of Serendip." He wrote, "As their highnesses traveled, they were always making discoveries, by accident and sagacity, of things they were not in quest of."

As I talked to people who had read my first book, CATS IN MY LIFE FROM GRANNY TO GINGER, I too kept making discoveries, although more by accident than sagacity, of stories I was not "in quest of," but which I delighted in hearing.

I now share with you the stories, both deliberate and accidental, in this collection of SERENDIPITY STORIES OF CATS AND THEIR PEOPLE.

Dedication

To the following friends who have made a difference in the lives of homeless animals I dedicate this book.

To Jennie who adopted Penny, Kathy, Angel Ole, Eric the Red, Melanie, Athena, and a whole line-up of other lucky cats.

To Marie and Maggie who have dedicated their lives to rescuing abandoned or abused cats and dogs.

And to Andrea who didn't leave it to someone else to help the lost dog who spent cold winter nights curled up under a pine tree.

Update on Cats in Residence

1. Theodore, Ginger and Skyehill Living

Theodore, Ginger and Skyehill Living

In my first book(CATS IN MY LIFE FROM GRANNY TO GINGER) Theodore and Ginger were the last on the scene. They were the two youngsters. Theodore, a big charcoal grey and white cat, had been a stray whose home was an abandoned building where a half open door hanging on broken hinges allowed access when he needed shelter or a place of escape. His hunting ground was the Nature Center behind the town house which my sister, Dagny, and I share. To judge by his heft, he hadn't fared too badly.

Ginger, part Siamese, arrived in a carrying case left beside our garage door one rainy Sunday afternoon. He came with a schizoid like personality, sometimes sweet and loving and at other times a biting, scratching terror.

Theodore, now about nine, and Ginger, four and a half, are still with us, a little older and wiser. Each is more secure as part of the family. Early animosity has changed into friendship. Theodore looks after Ginger as an older brother should.

One day Ginger wasn't feeling well. Miserable, he sought shelter under a couch. Theodore knew exactly what was needed. After giving him a good face washing and ear cleaning, he sat quietly at Ginger's side. When you're sick you need some special attention. Theodore

When you're sick you need special
attention. Theodore understood this.

understood that. Another day Ginger came home with an injured paw. He growled and whimpered in pain but later insisted he had to go out. "He won't go far. He's in too much pain," I murmured as I reluctantly opened the door and watched him limp down the deck stairs and out of sight.

While waiting for his return, I watched the ten o'clock news on TV and late night programs I hadn't seen in years. No Ginger appeared. Finally I went to bed. Tortured images of swooping owls and swift foxes targeting a limping Ginger moved through my uneasy sleep.

Morning came but no missing cat appeared. I ate breakfast while glancing often toward the sliding glass door. Sitting there looking for a cat who didn't appear was not productive. I cleared the table of the breakfast dishes, washed them and left them to dry in the dish rack. Next I went out into the garage to get some potting soil for an Aloe Vera plant that needed new space for all its off-shoots. I reached up to a storage shelf for the right size pot. Far back behind the clay pots were some empty boxes. From one of these Ginger's head appeared. He pulled himself free from his hiding place and, still favoring the sore foot, jumped down. He was ready to respond to our efforts to console him.

The part of Ginger's personality that causes him to hide when he is sick is definitely pure tabby! His Siamese ancestors knew better. A Canadian friend writes, "I have always liked Siamese because they tell me what is wrong. Woodstock jumped on the dining room table while we were eating and extended a paw in which a sliver was imbedded. Wendy, another time, walked to where I sat, retched, and deposited a tapeworm on my shoe, doing everything but looking up the vet's phone number."

Theodore will never be a lap sitter, but he now enjoys getting into bed to snuggle close as he purrs a loud contentment.

Ginger never overlooks an available lap. He also likes to cuddle. He goes one step beyond purring softly to prove his appreciation and affection. Have you ever had your face rubbed by a piece of wet, coarse sandpaper? I quickly place my hand between his tongue and my face. That's better. My hand can accept the loving licks and I don't have to hurt Ginger's feelings by pushing him away.

In November of 1991 winter arrived suddenly with 29 inches of snow and temperatures that dropped below zero. There was little time for any of us to adjust to the cold. I thought about the homeless cats who couldn't escape the cold as could Ginger and Theodore. After a ten minute excursion they scampered in, shaking cold feet and licking them warm. The next time the door was opened Ginger lifted a paw and shook it as he remembered how cold his feet were the last time he was out.

The snow and brisk air were intriguing. Theodore kept asking me to open the door so he could better view the winter scene and consider, while keeping his feet on warm carpeting, if he could possibly risk another outing. I gave his behind a gentle push. That settled it. He turned and ran to a chair warmed by the morning sun.

Deer in the Nature Center behind our town house were in their winter coats, a drab taupe which blends with the colors of the fall landscape. I looked at Ginger and saw that his coat too was showing the effects of shorter days and less intense sunlight. You've never heard of cats changing color? When in early summer I reported that it looked as if we would have to change Ginger's name because his ginger coloring was turning black, Dr Allen laughed and answered, "Well, if you say so."

On searching my books I found that some cats do undergo color change when exposed to a lot of sun and again in winter when days are shorter and they spend more time indoors. Color change is most commonly observed in the Siamese kitten who is born white and takes on coloration as he matures. Siamese in addition to responding to seasonal amounts and intensity of light continue to become darker as they age.

Ginger must have had one almost voiceless ancestor. His barely audible meow is totally inadequate. Never mind, body language gets him what he wants. A light spring on-to the buffet, or a repeated opening and closing of a cupboard door, is enough to get attention. If more is required, a book can be pulled off a shelf, or perhaps an art object can be pushed off a table. That will do it. Mission accomplished. Out he goes. Fortunately, as he grows older he usually refrains from the more extreme behavior to get his message across.

Theodore has a voice that would be the envy of an opera star. It has range; it has volume. It gets exercise enough to keep in top condition. We listen to his amazing variety of meows and try to understand what he is telling us.

What is there about cats that rewards us when we assume responsibility for their care? As I look back over the pages of a sparse journal which I kept rather haphazardly at the time Cali, Co, and Penny were the cats in residence, I find they were often in my thoughts.

Following are some aspects of their personalities which I enjoyed enough to record.

"A piece of black fur wrapped loosely around a sleeping cat becomes the essence of comfort and ease."

"I move about the kitchen preparing the evening meal. Three cats hear the opening of cupboards. Silently they join me, place themselves like statues knowing that they need not be loud to be heard."

Next it's Cali who makes it into the journal: "I settle into my upholstered Danish rocker to relax and watch television. But Cali stands and stares. With patience and persistence she waits until I concede and leave the chair to her. She usurps my place and curls up without a qualm. Cali has first rights. We both know that."

"'A place in the sun' we all agree is to have arrived. Each sunny day our cats find the 'place' near a window on softly carpeted floors. This is the ultimate in contentment."

"I envy you, pussycat. When you have eaten and curl up for a nap, surrounded by those you love and trust then for you there is no fear, no pain, no hunger in this world. God is indeed 'in his heaven and all's right with the world'."

When we moved to Skyehill in '82 we hoped that our luck would hold; that no ailurophobes would be our neighbors. The chances seemed good. Anyone checking would learn that there are few restrictions on pets in this development; our town homes attract either people who have animals, or who tolerate, even enjoy, neighbors' dogs and cats.

Recently Ginger overstepped bounds. One summer afternoon a city policeman rang the door bell. My sister, Dagny, went to the door. "Do you have a cat?" She answered that yes, we have two cats. An unidentified neighbor had called to complain that one of our cats was driving their dogs crazy by relaxing on the patio and looking through the sliding door at two frustrated dogs. Yes, that would be Ginger. Theodore would not be that brazen. What could be done about it? The policeman seemed as unable to come up with a good solution as my sister. "The cat was probably just sunning himself," he concluded reassuringly. It did seem possible that having two barking dogs, safely separated from him by glass, enhanced the experience from Ginger's point of view.

A few years after we had moved to Skyehill a new unit went up to the north of us and Katie Williams moved in with her daughter, Valerie, their Siamese cat, Tommy, and a white rabbit, Fluffy. After a few introductory spats and tangles Ginger and Theodore accepted Tommy into their territory. Tommy's south deck was a good place for absorbing the warmth of the sun. Theodore and Tommy could often be seen stretched out, side by side, on the warm boards as they relaxed together. Fluffy, when released from his hutch, could hop on the same deck with no danger of attack.

Ginger was sometimes allowed to slip into the house where he reportedly shared Tommy's dry food then went to the basement to use the litter box. Tommy sputtered and hissed and was not as amused as Valerie and Katy were.

Time passed. Tommy and Fluffy died. Valerie left home for Brandeis University. Tommy had been Valerie's friend since she was a very little girl. When she thought of home, Tommy was there, but when she returned for the holidays the reality was that Tommy did not greet her. Ginger's face at the door helped ease the loss. On one occasion, Valerie called to say that Ginger was with her. Would it be all right if she just opened her door to let him out when the visit was over? I said that would be just fine. Ginger would come to our sliding glass doors when he was ready to return.

After one Skyehill board meeting the small talk turned to pets. Our board president laughed, "We have the best pet. He's a part Siamese who comes over to be petted and played with. When he has visited long enough he goes to the door and reaches for the door knob. We have all the fun and none of the responsibility."

"Does he have a raccoon striped tail?" I asked. Sure enough, that was our Ginger who had been getting acquainted with yet another neighbor.

Ginger and Theodore have also found a new cat friend, Mack. Or rather Mack found them. Mack has been declawed. He was meant to be an indoor cat but had other ideas about that. First he was out on a leash. That just whetted his appetite for the excitement of green grass, trees, birds, and so many other wonderful sights and sounds. Not the least of his discoveries were Ginger and Theodore. Ginger pretends to ignore the slender black cat who follows him around at a respectful distance. Theodore and Mack touch noses and relax together stretched out on sidewalk or lawn.

Mack had missed seeing them for a few days when he spotted Theodore sitting on our deck with his back turned. He came running to grab Theodore around the neck, giving him a welcoming nip. Theodore responded with a start followed by a "So it's you again" look over his shoulder. At times Mack appears on our deck to look in through the glass door where his mentors and fellow explorers might be found.

Up to now Theodore and Ginger have dealt successfully with all the hazards of the neighborhood. They understand that they must stay out of the way of cars and automatically closing garage doors. Although Ginger still loves to get into a car to ride into the garage if the car door is opened and he is invited to jump in he gets shut in a neighbor's garage less often.

The Great Horned Owl and the fox still worry us. One morning the crows were noisily mobbing a Great Horned Owl in the basswood tree just the other side of the hurricane fence separating us from the Nature Center. Since night is the owl's time to be active, and since the cacophony of sound was pretty overwhelming even for the " tiger of the sky," the crows succeeded in routing him. As the owl headed north, the crows scattered and I gave thanks for their success. I look in wonder and admiration at the occasional red fox loping through the area. Both owl and fox remind me the cats could be in danger, particularly during night time wanderings.

The raccoons seem to be no threat, but we would like to draw the line at sharing a deck with them. On the west end of our wrap-around deck, which is fifteen steps up from the ground level, we had improvised a shelter for the cats just in case they needed some protection from rain or cold while waiting to be let into the house. The shelter was made of what was meant to be a covered litter box. We had slipped this into a plastic bag which is pulled shut with a draw string, leaving just enough of an opening for Theodore or Ginger to step in to enjoy the soft bedding provided.

One morning as we opened the door to let Theodore

in we noticed that he was staying as far away from the shelter as possible as he looked suspiciously towards it. I looked inside, also apprehensive of what I might see. Looking back at me were a pair of masked eyes set in a small triangular face. I shook the box, hoping the animal would become frightened and leave. No response. Dagny moved the box to the far end of the deck, still with no response. Three days passed. Each time the box was checked, day or night, the raccoon was inside. For night checking we kept a flash-light handy. By now even our noses picked up the sharp, wild smell of raccoon as we moved past. For the cats, the smell must have meant their familiar deck was invaded and taken over.

The fourth morning we glanced out the glass door to the east end of the deck and were startled to see a small raccoon stretched out absorbing the rays of the bright sun. As we watched, he sat up slowly and began using his tiny, finger-like feet to wash his wounds. Most visible to us was the large open wound on his head. Raccoons are territorial animals. Had this small creature invaded territory already marked off by an older and stronger animal? We also noted that one end of the deck had been used as a toilet. All those stairs were still too much work, but he had it all figured out.

Now that we were beginning to understand that our deck and box shelter had been selected for rest and recuperation we were less apprehensive that Little Rascal had moved in permanently. No longer did we have uneasy visions of a whole family of raccoons establishing headquarter on our deck. One little raccoon, in desperate need, had remembered the shelter discovered during more tranquil night time adventuring.

Each morning, which is bed time for raccoons, we

Theodore was giving the shelter a wide berth as he looked suspiciously towards it.

looked into the box. One morning we found it empty. "Good, he's no longer using the box. Today we dismantle it and store it in the garage."

"No," Dagny answered uneasily, "They're predicting rain. We'll give him one more night." This went on for some days. The cats moved cautiously around the covered box, which they had to pass each time they came or went. Sometimes Theodore would stop to peer through the opening, then draw back quickly. Finally we found the "den" had not been used for two days in succession. It was dismantling time. We trust Little Rascal is making it in the woods.

We look at out two fat cats and hope they are now too heavy and evasive to be tackled by denizens of the area who are known to include an occasional cat in their diets.

A partisan friend says she is certain Theodore and Ginger are Republicans. May the "fat cats" slim down (I know, I know, we have to open fewer cans) and continue to enjoy life in health and safety for many years to come.

The Gift of Nine Lives

2. Cat Fact and Fancy

Cat Fact and Fancy

Fact: The cat, unlike the dog and horse, walks or runs by moving the front and back legs on one side, then the front and back legs on the other side. Only the camel and the giraffe move in a similar way.

Fancy: Cats have nine lives. This fancy has a long history which may date back to ancient Egypt. Thousands of cat mummies have been discovered as well as mouse mummies, presumably to provide food for the cats.

About 4000 years ago Egyptians believed there was a cat-headed goddess. They called her Pasht or Bastet. Some now think the name "Puss" is derived from Pasht. She was thought to have nine lives. Because the cat was identified with Pasht, the nine lives legend rubbed off and cats too were credited with nine lives.

Through all the ups and downs, ranging from sacred to tools of the devil, cats have seemed determined to enjoy life, or to suffer through with a tenacity that reinforced the myth and kept it going. Henry Beston in THE OUTERMOST HOUSE tells of coast guard at Cape Cod boarding a wrecked ship the morning after the storm. In the dead captain's cabin they found a chilled canary hunched up on his perch and a grey cat calmly waiting. The bird died while being taken ashore but the cat called on all remaining lives and lived to "found a dynasty to carry on his name." The following stories make me wonder if the legend may have something to it.

A couple years ago, when we in Minnesota had one of our extremely cold spells, 20 below in fact, an elderly lady called the next door neighbor whom she often turned to when she needed help. This time she had stepped out to pick up her morning paper and saw, as she thought, a dead cat who seemed frozen stiff. Would he pick up the body and place it in the garbage? Thinking he might as well get that chore taken care of the neighbor ran out to rid the scene of the frozen cat carcass. As he bent to pick it up he thought he heard a faint meow. He listened more closely. The meow was repeated. Taking the cat to his basement he wrapped it in warm towels. Gradually, as he watched, the body thawed, the eyes opened and the cat sat up to examine unfamiliar surroundings. The rescuer later observed that the only permanent damage seemed to be to the tail. The ears, which are usually the first to suffer frost bite, were not damaged. At the time I heard this story the cat had not been brought to the vet. I don't know the end of either the "tale" or the "tail." Did the tail fall off, or have to be amputated? Of one thing I am certain; there went one of the nine lives, maybe even two.

Another story goes back to the times when sick cats were not as likely to end their days on the veterinarian's examining table. This particular cat had been looking and acting very ill. Jack, whose cat this was, decided it would be merciful to end this miserable existence. The most humane way he could think of was to ask the drug store pharmacist for enough chloroform to kill a cat. A sturdy cardboard box found in the basement served as the "death chamber." He applied a chloroform soaked towel to the face, closed the box and, when all movement inside ceased, he left.

The next day, hating the task, he walked slowly down the steps to the basement, knelt by the box and forced his reluctant hands to undo the cover. Reaching inside he removed the small towel which had been soaked with chloroform. Instead of the lifeless animal he had so dreaded to see, Ross was lying as if asleep. As the light and air entered the box, he uncurled his body, focused his eyes, shook his head, and jumped easily out of the box. After sitting for a moment, seemingly to get his bearings, Ross stretched and ran lightly up the steps to the kitchen. Jack hurried after. Ross was already sitting by the empty food dish which had of late been of no interest. He looked up expectantly. Jack filled the dish and watched in wonder as Ross emptied the container. It became evident Jack's cat was likely to enjoy health for some years to come.

It sometimes happens that a cat who is outdoors on a cold night discovers that there is some warmth under the hood of a car. If he does not awaken and leave before the car is started, that will very likely be his last sleep. All nine lives are used up with the whirl of the fly wheel. The particular cat whose story was told to me escaped being cut up and was instead overcome by carbon monoxide.

Bernard had arrived home late the night before. The weather was cold and blustery. He quickly closed the garage door and entered the house. Jeff, his son, asked if he had seen the cat outside. No, Bernard hadn't seen him.

"You better go out and prop the service door open,"

The cat sat up, and looking refreshed, greeted his would-be assasin with a puzzled look.

Bernard suggested. "It's cold out there, but he can sleep in his box in the garage when he gets home."

In the morning still no cat. In preparation for starting the car for the trip to work, Bernard remembered he needed to fill the container of window washing fluid. Bottle in hand, he lifted the hood. There to his horror lay the cat, apparently dead. What could he do with this dead cat? Everyone else had already left for school or work. He was late and needed to leave too.

"I'll break the news tonight," he thought. "For now, I can't do anything for him." He lifted the lid of the garbage can and placed the cat into it right on top of a plastic bag which was tied and ready for disposal.

That evening Bernard was the first one home. He hadn't been able to get his mind off that dead cat. He lifted the lid of the garbage can. To his astonishment and relief out jumped kitty. That evening kitty was kept in the house. The family suddenly realized how much they loved their cat.

Minnesota cold can kill, and so can desert heat. The Bensons had recently moved from Minnesota to Las Vegas. They made the trip by car during cool April weather. Julie, Nathan, the three kids, and Jacob, the cat, enjoyed the trip in their spacious van. Jacob was a good traveler. When they stopped for the night at a motel, the cat nosed around the room to become familiar with the new smells then curled up for the night in the bathroom sink. After arriving at their Las Vegas home, they spent several months getting settled.

Meanwhile the children were studying the history of the area and learning about the different kinds of life in a climate so different from Minnesota's. Beatty, Nevada, they read, just 120 miles from Las Vegas, lies in the mid-

Twelve hours later the lid of the can was lifted. Out jumped Kitty.

dle of the border zone where the Mojave overlaps the Great Basin and where a tiny triangle of the Death Valley National Monument edges into Nevada. Beatty has a history of gold mines and dreams of becoming the "Chicago of the West." A trip to Beatty seemed like a good way to begin exploring their new state.

The kids insisted that Jacob should be included on the excursion. They had no air conditioning in the car, but if they traveled during the cool morning hours they could get along. Somehow, it got to be nine before they took off. After an hour of driving, the desert heat was making the car unbearable. The cat was not in a carrier. If the window was opened, he struggled to jump out. At other times he lay on his back and panted,

They finally stopped near a growth of cacti, sagebrush, and juniper mesquite; all vegetation which they recognized from their studies. Perhaps here they could drink some of the water they had with them and recover enough to continue to Beatty where an air-conditioned motel room was waiting. Jacob crawled under a stand of sagebrush where the air was a bit cooler. When it was time to move on Jacob refused to come out. Julie covered her hand with a cloth and pulled the fighting, protesting animal from under his shelter. She wrapped him in a wet towel and they completed the journey with a new respect for the desert and its power. Heat and dehydration may have placed a strain on all of them, but Jacob was the only one credited with having a threatened life to spare.

Yes, it's still great to have nine lives to draw on. As Dr. Allen, our vet, commented while treating Theodore, a peace loving cat who gets wounds on tail or hind quarter as he beats a retreat, "It's a dangerous world out there."

But the lucky, well cared for cat now has the advantage of veterinary care.

Veterinary medicine is nothing new. It was found in Babylon and Egypt as early as 2000 BC. It wasn't squandered on cats however but was reserved for "beasts of burden." Even for them veterinary medicine all but disappeared during the dark and Middle Ages. It wasn't until the 1940s and '50s that cats began to receive much veterinary care.

Another story seems to belong more to tales of navigation, determination, and intelligence; but there are some nine lives implications here too. Sigrid, who lives in South Minneapolis near Minnehaha Creek, was enjoying her backyard one mellow October day. A soft wind rustled the fallen leaves which were beginning to cover the lawn with many patches of color.

Suddenly Sigrid was startled by the sight of a cat stretched out and resting on her lawn. He was a large, sturdy cat with tabby markings and a long, thick coat. Sig noted that he resembled a Maine Coon. He looked well cared for. Upon becoming aware of Sig he arose and slowly with no apparent fear approached her. Sig hurried into the house to bring food which he bolted. In consideration of her four house cats she didn't invite him in. Instead she took him to the garage where she cut the bindings on a bale of straw she had bought in preparation for bedding in some of her plants. She arranged the straw as a mattress and covered it with an old jacket. She also left a dish of water and one bowl of dry food. Next she went into the house and checked the want ads. Seeing no ad, Sig ran a lost cat ad herself.

Meanwhile on the other side of town 17 miles from Sig's house Bonnie was frantically searching lost and found sections of local papers. Her cat, Mosef Ralph VonDruska, was missing. Bonnie and her husband had recently moved to Minneapolis from Chicago. Bonnie, a dance school owner, had arranged to return to the Windy City at two week intervals until her dance school commitments were completed. Her husband would remain in their new home and agreed to care for the cat. The problem was that Mosef, the cat, and the husband had little time for or interest in each other. The cat left his new home with plans, it seemed, to follow Bonnie to Chicago. Sig and her ad meant Mosef didn't have to go all the way. Instead he achieved his aim of finding Bonnie after completing only the first 17 miles of his treck. Cat and owner, having found each other, left Sig's with thanks and appreciation.

Two weeks later the entire scenario was repeated, including the ad in the paper, the responding call from Bonnie, and the glad reunion. This time Sig had become wary. She carefully wrote down name and telephone number. Although surely she would not need it.

Two weeks passed and, like a recurring dream, there was Mosef again, apparently heading for Chicago. Unlike Bonnie, he had to go on foot. After the first seventeen miles Mosef needed a rest and refueling stop. Sig seemed in the right place for the break. She came through with food and a place to sleep. Since Bonnie had also turned up there, it made good sense to stick with the original travel plan.

Fortunately Bonnie had fulfilled her Chicago dance commitments. With winter on its way, walking to Chicago, even with well planned food and rest stops,

After the first seventeen
miles Mosef needed a
rest and a refueling stop.

would have required great care if Mosef's nine lives were to prove an adequate number.

Just to make sure there were no travel plans in Mosef's head, he was grounded for the winter. After all the excitement of travel, Mosef was pretty bored with nothing to do but to eat, sleep and check on winter birds through the window. He did have great memories and had plenty of time to dictate this letter to Sig:

"Hi, dear friend, I didn't have much of a chance to get acquainted with Mitz, Homestead, Chugger, Orphan Annie, and Kitty 500, but I do get lonesome for all the excitement when we got together. Otherwise I'm quite happy in my new home. Bonnie says I have to spend the winter indoors. Come spring I may be "on the road again" to visit you. I love traveling.

Your loving sometime son,

Moe"

Library Cats

3. Buffalo Bill Lives

4. Regal Reggie

5. And More Library Cats

Buffalo Bill Lives

Upon entering the Detroit Lakes Public Library in North Western Minnesota, you will see to your left a large and attractive children's room. After taking in the stacks of books, the tables, and the quiet hum of children browsing, your eye may travel to a clay sculpture of a cat sitting on a black painted wooden base backed by large windows which allow the outside world to become a part of the setting. On the base are these words: "I am the cat—Comrade of waif and king. At home in palace and peasant cot. I am the cat!" by Harriet Amundsen. On the side is a small plaque stating: "In memory of George and Milla Peoples. Placed here by friends and family, October, 1962. Sculptured in clay by Mabel Peoples Swanson, especially for the children's library."

In this sculpting, known only as" The Library Cat," lives the spirit of "Buffalo Bill." How did it happen that this cat, who started life as a homeless stray, lives on in the Detroit Lakes Public Library?

It was a beautiful fall day when Mibs (Mabel Peoples Swanson) and Walter decided on a 200 mile trip from Minneapolis to Detroit Lakes before cold and winter would make the drive less pleasant to see Mibs' mother and father.

When they arrived in Elk River they pulled in to the parking lot behind a restaurant where they had stopped many times before. They paused to admire the fall colors

31

The Library Cat

I am the cat
Comrade of waif and King
At home in palace and peasant cot,
I am the cat!

in the weed and brush covered slope behind the parked cars. A young cat came walking towards them. They noted his long, fine fur which in turn had a coat of nettles and burrs.

"Poor kitty needs someone to help him get rid of all those burrs," commented Mibs as they continued into the restaurant.

"Who does that cat out in back belong to?" Walter asked the waitress as she found them a table.

"Oh, he's just a wild cat who hangs out around here. We don't like to feed him or we would probably get stuck with him. And he's not friendly. You can't pick him up. If you try he fights to get away."

Mibs and Walter ordered coffee and a hamburger each, then added, "And one hamburger with no seasoning for the wild one." Well, customers must be catered to so the order was filled.

A half hour later they walked out with the third unseasoned hamburger, half afraid that the homeless one would have left. But no, he was there waiting to accept their attention and to not only accept, but to inhale the hamburger. Mibs stooped down to pet him and exclaimed, "No wonder he fights when he's picked up! Nettles and burrs are not just *on* his fur. They're imbedded! It must really hurt when a hand presses them into his skin." The cat allowed an on the spot de-nettling. Enough at least so that Mibs could pick him up and place him on her lap to join them on their trip to Detroit Lakes.

Mibs recalls, "I often sing as I ride along, so I sang to the cat as he sat quietly on my lap." Soon she heard a low purring accompaniment to her voice. Later Mibs wondered if Buffalo Bill remembered this first ride and the soothing, reassuring sound of her voice. Through the years, whenever she sang, Buffalo Bill looked up into her face and, if she was sitting down, jumped into her lap to accompany her with that amazing purring instrument. "Perhaps he thought that was my way of purring," Mibs muses.

As they continued their trip Mibs studied her cat more carefully. She had noticed his short, "cobby" legs. Now she admired the luxuriant white ear feathers on otherwise black ears and the long white whiskers. She commented to Walter that his eye make-up was equal to that of the proverbial Queen of Sheba. A flourishing white bib and white toes added distinction to his basic grey coloring. The feather light body under all that long fur was that of a very young cat who had been having a hard time making a living.

Upon their arrival the new pet soon won the hearts of Mibs' parents. Being confined to a house didn't seem to be a problem. By the time they left for home he was secure with his new friends and again purred his contentment as he curled up to sleep in Mibs' lap.

Back home in Minnetonka their two dogs eyed the new addition with suspicion. Boots was a black and white Spaniel. Dal seemed to be the best of at least two breeds. His coloring was white, spotted with black like a Dalmation. There also seemed to be a lot of German Shorthair Pointer in his genes.

Eyeing the dogs uneasily the newcomer backed into a corner of the kitchen. "Enough for today," Mibs concluded. She escorted Boots and Dal to the basement for the night. Tomorrow they would give getting acquainted another try.

After a few days of watching and offering cautious

overtures of friendship, both cat and dogs relaxed and began to accept that they all belonged. Boots had come as a puppy and believed the luxuries of his home to be the inalienable right of every animal. Dal had found Mibs and Walter by pure chance when he staggered in, hungry and desperate, one fall day some years earlier. Perhaps he and the young cat shared similar memories and congratulated each other on their good fortunes. At night Buffalo Bill soon insisted on squeezing his body into a bed already a tight squeeze for Dal's considerable size. Dal did his best to accommodate.

Peace and harmony now prevailed inside, but something had to be done about protecting the neighborhood cats. A cat who makes his living hunting needs a large territory. Other cats cut down on available food and are not tolerated. This new cat looked the territory over and began beating up on peaceful neighborhood cats! Mibs and Walter studied his pugnacious chin and aggressive behavior and decided neutering would help. Their vet agreed.

For a time the new cat remained nameless, then they settled on "Buffalo Bill." His namesake was a hunter and a fighter, but he was also a showman and a hero in many a dime novel in his time. Ingri and Edgar d'Aulaire say in their child's book, BUFFALO BILL: "He was full of cheer and good stories. He was seldom tired and never afraid. When nobody else dared ride with warnings to outlying forts, he rode alone." Yes, "Buffalo Bill" seemed a suitable name for the many faceted cat. Admittedly, Buffalo Bill the frontiersman needed a crash course in respect for the Native Americans and their culture, but

Mibs and Walter decided to go with the romanticized version.

In time neutering did result in a reduced territorial area but "Bill" continued to insist that the yard around the house be reserved for him and the dogs. Boots agreed. Sometimes when Buffalo Bill was out at night he would get involved in a yodeling cat fight in the lower yard. Mibs or Walter then quickly opened the door so Boots could tear out of the house barking wildly. Buffalo Bill would hear him coming and retreat while Boots shagged the interloper out of the yard. They then strolled back into the house, no doubt congratulating each other on a job well done.

One night Buffalo Bill joined Boots in the chase. In his excitement Boots confused Buffalo Bill with the enemy and tore after him. This race went on for about 30 feet before it dawned on them that there was something wrong with this scenario. Both stopped in their tracks, looked chagrined, and slowly walked home to where Walter, much amused, waited to usher them in so the rest of the night could be spent in peace.

During one night of adventuring Buffalo Bill had a very close call and Walter got a black eye. It was a warm spring evening; warm enough so that an unscreened bedroom window had been left open just enough to allow the cat to enter without having to wake Mibs or Walter. Suddenly through this window shot Buffalo Bill, with feet that hit hard, over the bed, heading for the far corner of the room. One foot landed squarely on Walter's eye.

Possibly an owl or a hawk, the feathered world's revenge on feline predators, had nearly ended Buffalo Bill's life. Other dangers he could have met head on but if danger swoops down on a six foot wing span a cat ducks it any way he can. The open window made escape possible. Walter had the task of explaining to the folks at work how he got his black eye. His explanation, "My cat stomped on my eye," did not seem very credible at the office.

Buffalo Bill had his pensive moments. One evening Mibs looked out of her kitchen window and was enchanted by the sight of their cat sitting quietly, lighted by the back yard lamp, as he followed with his eyes the large, soft flakes floating down, covering both him and all surfaces around him. Just one more wonder and marvel in his world.

Buffalo Bill was not exclusively an "outdoor" cat. He also led a full and more civilized life inside the house as companion and friend to Mibs, Walter, and their friends. The kitchen was small so Buffalo Bill took as little space as possible while he supervised activities. He commonly sat on a stool, paws tucked in, as he watched Mibs with her kitchen chores of cleaning, canning, or food preparation.

He seemed to understand when company was expected. Then he would sit on a desk which allowed him to watch for their arrival. Mibs insists he wore a smile of anticipation. Most special was Kristine, a little girl who was Buffalo Bill's very own company. She rigged up a shoe box with a string for pulling the box from room to room. Buffalo Bill jumped in and out, the box being too small for him to fit into, like a stunt man in a circus.

The breakfast nook was a favorite spot for Mibs to set up her typewriter to get some work done. Buffalo Bill was quick to hear the clatter of keys and report for duty as an assistant. The kitten on the keys problem was

Buffalo Bill was quick to hear the clatter of the keys and report for duty as an assistant.

solved when Walter remembered the old typewriter he had stored in the garage. This they set up across from Mibs and Buffalo Bill typed happily on his own typewriter with Mibs there to unscramble the keys as needed.

When typewriters weren't out he could play with one of the toys kept in his drawer, the bottom drawer of the kitchen cupboard. Or perhaps the tap in the bath tub could be turned on "just a trickle" so he could dab at it, study the moving water as he tried to figure out where all this was coming from. Finally he would leave the tub, sneezing to get the water out of his nose, as he began the big job of licking feet dry.

This was the good life. He was definitely no longer living off the land, but rather "off the cans." It was special cat food mostly, but at noon he often joined Mibs and Walter for a taste of soup, or for a sardine when a can of "King Oscar, Silver in Oil" was opened. No other brand, thanks, and just one sardine from a freshly opened can. This piece he carefully licked until it was completely free of oil, then the sardine itself was eaten.

For twelve wonderful years Buffalo Bill lived with Mibs and Walter, enriching their lives; then disaster struck. A leashed dog, out for a walk, saw Buffalo Bill in his front yard and broke loose to attack. He grabbed the cat by his back before the screams and frantic intervention of his owner could stop him.

Mibs sighed her relief when she later checked her cat and saw no blood, only messed up hair. He seemed to have escaped serious injury.

After some days, however, Buffalo Bill was clearly not well. When Mibs found him stretched out on the cool cement floor of the pump room she knew something was very wrong. In distress, she called Walter. As he picked Buffalo Bill up for his last ride he agreed that there seemed to be little life left in their cat. The vet concurred that there was internal injury and that a lethal injection should bring a merciful end. Buffalo Bill died while held in Walter's arms.

Mibs remembers that long after he died she would walk around the stool in her kitchen as if he were still on it. "His presence was powerful and lingered with us." Mibs is an artist. What is in her heart is expressed through her hands. As she worked with a piece of clay she formed with loving fingers the cat she and Walter missed so much. Thus it happened that Buffalo Bill still lives surrounded by children and people whom he loved.

Children stop to stroke and hug the cat who sits on his black platform, which brings him to eye level with them as they pass to find a book. One little boy was heard to ask him, "What book shall I read today?"

Buffalo Bill does indeed live on in this small town library, reincarnated as "The Library Cat."

Regal Reggie

"The quality of mercy is twice bless'd. It blesseth him that gives, and him that takes." When Mark Twain used this quotation from Shakespeare in introducing THE PRINCE AND THE PAUPER he was not thinking of cats. However Mark Twain liked cats and would, I am certain, agree that not only Reggie but rescuer, Phyllis Lahti, qualifies for the blessing which "droppeth as the gentle rain from heaven." I think he might also concede that Reggie, who began life as a "pauper", needed only a chance, as did Tom Canty, to show truly royal behavior. Following is the story of how Reggie became a princely library cat and also how he came to be sent packing:

Phyllis was at that time living in a trailer in a small northern Minnesota town. In the vicinity there were a number of homeless cats for whom she often provided food. She paid special attention to a little grey tabby with a white front and white paws.

One day early in March winter weather returned. The radio in the work room of the public library, where Phyllis was librarian, interrupted scheduled programs to warn of closed roads and driving hazards. Phyllis peered through the window. There wasn't much she could see. No doubt about it, a Minnesota blizzard was raging through the area making homes and highways almost invisible. She hadn't seen a patron for hours.

School closings were announced at regular intervals. Phyllis also decided on an early closing.

Because the day had begun windy and threatening Phyllis felt well prepared for whatever a blizzard might offer. Slipping into her wool lined coat, she pulled the hood up over her head, tied the scarf, pulled on warm boots and heavy mittens and looked forward to an invigorating mile and a half to her trailer home. She had visions of spending the evening curled up on her couch with a good book and her two cats. It wasn't too bad a prospect.

Wind had whipped the already fallen snow from one side of the street to the other. Some compacted into drifts solid enough to be walked on. Where the sidewalk ran was anybody's guess. Familiar landmarks were taking on strange shapes or were disappearing entirely. Phyllis was glad that she did not have to face into the storm. The wind at her back urged her on at a fast pace.

Arriving at her trailer she paused to survey the landscape while wondering where the homeless cats were finding refuge. Pitting her strength against the wind, she unlocked the door, held it open long enough to enter the house, then pulled the door shut behind her.

As she pushed back her hood and prepared to take off her boots, Phyllis heard a strange howling outside. Cautiously she again opened the door. There stood a desperately cold, snow covered cat howling for his life. She recognized the little grey tabby with the white bib and paws. He had come for help from the one person in the community he knew to be a friend. Phyllis picked him up and quickly closed the door to shut out the storm and placed him on the floor while she finished removing her snow encrusted clothes.

No longer expressing loudly his pain and fear the cat allowed Phyllis to again pick him up and examine him. Skin had been torn away from his paws leaving open sores. He had a badly damaged ear. Phyllis filled a small bowl with warm water to which she added hydrogen peroxide. Using a length of cotton bandage from her first aid kit she washed his paws and cleaned his torn ear. He was a trusting cat and accepted help gratefully. Before the evening was over Phyllis knew she now had three cats. "Reggie" had found a home.

The first few months after his rescue that stormy day Reggie lived with Phyllis and her two cats, Dudley, a Siamese, and Whitney, a white and marmalade cat. In time Reggie's paws recovered completely but he was left with a diminished sense of hearing and sometimes shakes his head as if that ear is causing him discomfort. Phyllis has not heard him howl since that desperate day in 1985.

Whitney had no great objection to a third cat around, but Dudley let it be known he would shed no tears if Reggie should move to another home.

Reggie evidently recognized that he was on probation and made himself as small and obscure as possible. He adjusted to the litter pan with no problems although this was probably the first such convenience in his lifetime.

Phyllis describes Reggie as follows: "Early abandonment has left him slightly aloof although, when he responds, he purrs softly and nuzzles. As soft to touch as he is to look at, he gives attention to grooming and appreciates having his fur brushed and combed, assisting by rolling over to get the job done right. His voice is modulated to low pitched meows that sound sweetly. He has the integrity, reliability, and predictability befitting a 'gentleman'. One thing can break his reserve—the smell of cod. I think he would give a paw for a piece of cod, or most any kind of fish. Sometimes a catnip mouse makes him a bit giddy."

Phyllis listened to Dudley's views on the matter (who can avoid listening when a Siamese airs his complaints?) and considered Reggie's personality. It did seem that he would make a great library cat. And Dudley was wearing her down.

Phyllis decided to give it a try. Reggie was introduced to a new life in the library. He was given a bed in the basement furnace room where he slept in an old moth-eaten upholstered brown chair. He endured with patience the darkness and shabbiness relieved by explorations in the basement book room. Mornings when the library was not open to the public Reggie spent in the office.

"It cannot be said that the part-time staff embraced him whole-heartedly; indeed, one older staff person thought Reggie would never adjust to the library. Or perhaps it was the other way around. In time he seemed to win respect, and the doubtful one brought him fresh fish from summer outings."

Phyllis continues: "After six months he had been promoted to the library office, sleeping in a wicker basket acquired for him. He served his post steadily, quietly, and discreetly, like an English butler, perhaps. In those early days anywhere beyond the library office was out of bounds. He accepted this. On weekends I often picked Reggie up for a ride in the country or for an outing to a park. He liked to view the receding scenery from the back window as he stood up and placed his front feet on the backrest of the seat he occupied. Or I would visit him in the library, taking him outside to run on the small library grounds. He loved the chance to climb the trees and stalk the moving blades of grass. Evenings, when the library was closed, I sometimes stopped in to give him a pat and a hug. As I prepared to leave, he would jump onto the window sill and we both looked out at the evening traffic with its display of moving lights. This became a ritual."

Slowly and cautiously Reggie was allowed to expand his duties as "Library Cat." The wicker basket was moved to the Children's reading room. During cold evenings Phyllis placed the basket near a radiator to make this a cozy place for Reggie's frequent cat naps.

Children who had noticed Reggie sometimes stopped in after school to see him, small children and teenagers alike. For them Reggie was his gentle self, allowing his admirers to pet him and talk to him. One day a little boy asked for "Prince." When Phyllis, puzzled, said they did not have a Prince in the library, he became upset and shouted, "Yes, you do!" Fortunately, at that moment Reggie walked by. The boy excitedly pointed to him, "There's Prince!" One of the volunteers also recognized Reggie's royal qualities. She referred to him as "Regal Reggie." Yes, regal, but not pompous or arrogant. "He seemed grateful for everything that was done for him," Phyllis recalls.

For three years Reggie served his post well, adding warmth, color, and life to the small town library. During this time Phyllis moved ten miles to a farm house which she rented from the owner who had built a newer home a short distance from this, their original home. Phyllis received permission to share this home with Dudley and Whitney. They all enjoyed the quiet country life with no lack of space either indoors or outdoors. This was the perfect place for Phyllis to pursue a writing project she had found difficult to fit into her day.

Phyllis began noticing a small, timid cat who wandered around the farm-yard without seeming to belong to any-one. She asked Betsy and George, from whom she rented, if they knew whose cat this was. They too had noticed her and assumed she was just another stray, probably from a nearby farm. Phyllis, a soft touch for homeless cats, named the cat "Sadie" and thought of Reggie. If she could bring Sadie to join him in the library, Reggie's evenings and nights would be less lonely.

To Reggie Sadie's arrival may have seemed most of all an invasion of territory. However he tolerated the intru-sion of the small, beige and white charmer with the almond shaped eyes, who wanted so much to please everyone.

Eventually Reggie decided the new cat was at least useful as a warm body in the basket when the evenings turned cold in the drafty library. During library hours Sadie was restricted to the office, often sleeping in one of the cabinets where it was warmest. Reggie remained the kingpin in the children's room.

Reggie had story hour responsibilities. At times he was the central figure who inspired children to tell their stories of a cat they knew, lived with, or had read about. At other times he blended in with the children and lis-tened to, or slept through, the story hour as just another participant.

When two matrons complained of the aggressive intent they attributed to Reggie as he eyed birds outside

Reggie had story hour responsibilities and at times he was the central figure.

the window and played his game of hunter stalking prey in the jungle, a warning bell should have been heard.

This small town was the center for a large farming community. Many adults using the library were not accustomed to an indoor cat. One patron (who may have visited the library three or four times over a period of ten years) contacted the Board and complained that seeing a cat in the library made her "almost hysterical." There was no time to rally support for Reggie and Sadie. The Board quickly agreed that the cats must go. Where they went was no concern of theirs. Thus ended Reggie's career as a library cat, and poor Sadie had hardly made a start.

Phyllis remembered her landlord's hesitation when she had asked permission to keep two cats in her rented farm house. She couldn't risk approaching the owner with a request to add two more cats to the household. She saw no alternative. The cats would have to be smuggled in. They would become contraband cats. Their living quarters could be the upstairs rooms. Their "cage" would be spacious and light, but a lonely place with no children and no visitors. For only a brief time each Sunday morning Reggie and Sadie could stretch their limbs and breath the fresh air of the farm yard. At that time George and Betsy were sure to be attending church services.

For nine months Reggie and Sadie lived their secret lives on the second floor. They saw no one but Phyllis. They watched the sun rise and set through their upstairs windows. They chattered at the birds who were free to fly or to rest in the trees. But they were warm, and they were fed and loved.

"And then we moved to Moorhead, Minnesota,"

Two matrons complained of wicked
thoughts in Reggie's head.

Phyllis relates. "And the cats are all on one floor, in their own home at last; so they have to get along, and they do. Now I see more of Reggie and Sadie than I ever did. They are happier. They may now go out each evening for about 15-20 minutes, then are ushered into the garage from where I call them into the house. These gentle and dependable cats like routine, and are appreciative of comforts that they never knew until they joined me. I'm beginning to take them for granted."

Have you been wondering throughout this story how it can be that two homeless tabby cats, accustomed to moving freely as they hunted and scrounged for a living, can gracefully sacrifice freedom in exchange for all the restrictions imposed on them in order to qualify for food, love, and security? It happens quite often that a cat, who has had a very difficult time surviving, decides the great out-of-doors can easily be exchanged for the comforts of a home. The memory of the pain and struggle lingers and the cat adjusts to an amazing degree. Reggie and Sadie changed life styles with few objections. They purr their contentment when, after nightmarish dreams of cold, starvation, hurt, and rejection, they wake up to the comforts of life with Phyllis.

And More Library Cats

Although Reggie is not the first cat to be part of a library staff, it can be said he was the first associate member of The Library Cat Society founded in 1987 by Phyllis Lahti. Members of LCS support the view that librarians, books, and cats were made for each other. Their quarterly newsletter testifies to the love and respect librarians, their staffs and, in most cases, the public have for the library cats and the contributions made by their presence.

As a charter member of the Society Reggie takes second place to no one. True, Reggie was fired from his post; but you know how things are today if you don't have the protection of a union.

Baker and Taylor might however hold the record for impressive lineage and privileged beginnings. They are two Scottish Fold cats who live in the Douglas County Public Library in Minden, Nevada, about forty miles south of Reno.

How did they come to be? What I mean to say, and to explain, is how they came to be born with ears that fold over giving them a strangely appealing look with rounder faces than can be found in other breeds of cats.

In 1961 William Ross saw Susie on a Perthsire, Scotland farmyard. She was a pure white cat whose ears were folded down onto her head rather than standing up in the normal positon. He kept a watchful eye on Susie and her off-spring. Two years later his patient waiting was rewarded. Susie gave birth to two folded ear kittens. Ross bought one of these kittens, registered it, and named it Snooks. Then breeders took over and began selecting for this attention-getting bent over ear. As to color, it runs the gamut. Baker is blue and white, while Taylor is a brown and white tabby.

Now that you know why Baker and Taylor have these folded ears, I'll share how they came to be library cats. A new library was being planned for Douglas County. Mice nibbling their way through valuable holdings had been a problem in the location about to be abandoned. The new facility was to be built in what had up to now been an alfalfa field and might have even more problems with rodents. It seemed wise to consider how to keep field mice from looking for food and shelter in the new library.

Yvonne Saddler and Jan Louch, director and assistant director of the Douglas County Library respectively, saw this as a valid reason for acquiring a Scottish Fold like the one they had fallen in love with at a recent cat show.

It was now just a matter of finding a "Fold" with the right personality for life in a library setting. This quest was turned over to friends, Bill and Brenda Kinnuen, operators of a cattery in Pacific Grove, California. They suggested that an offspring of "Big Red," who was known for his docile personality, might fill the bill. Voila! There sat ten month old Clint Eastman, relative of Big Red, waiting to be adopted.

All agreed Clint's name was not appropriate for a round, furry ball of a cat. Something better had to be found. Also the name should be library related and

Baker and Taylor must hold the record
for impressive lineage and privileged beginnings.
("Inspired by the famous Baker and Taylor Library cats.")

unique enough so that it would not be shared with any other library cat. Since Baker & Taylor are wholesale book dealers who have a division office in Reno, it was decided that "Baker" would be suitable. Also, this name left room for expansion, as a companion cat was already contemplated.

Bill Hartman, Baker & Taylor's Director of Western Sales, was advised of the honor bestowed upon his company and alerted to the fact that Jan and Yvonne were saving up "out of their measly paychecks" to buy a companion for Baker. The second cat would be named Taylor. Bill, a man of vision who knows good publicity when he sees it, promptly responded by acknowledging that the least Baker & Taylor could do in recognition of this honor was to pay for Taylor when he was located.

A year old nephew of Baker became the cat of choice. Thus it happened that Taylor came to live with Uncle Baker in the Douglas County Public Library and that 30,000 libraries or book stores have posters of two flat eared cats posing solemnly as "part symbol, part mascot, part goodwill ambassadors, and part spokesmen" for Baker & Taylor books.

To keep things from getting dull, Jan reports, Baker and Taylor, who are now eleven and ten respectively, have entertained, or been entertained by a stray raven, a goose, an occasional grasshopper and some spiders, as well as guide dogs. These visitors they take in stride. But a visiting elephant! Picturing two little cats looking at an elephant at close range I am reminded of the old Indian legend of the blind man who was taken to "see" an elephant. The blind man "reached out his eager hand, and felt about the knee. 'What this most wondrous beast is like is mighty plain to see. Tis clear enough the elephant is very like a tree'." Baker and Taylor probably saw, not one tree, but four large, moving trees.

During more tranquil times Baker and Taylor are hosts to children and young people who come to the library to read, study, or perhaps to have the joy of a pet which they cannot have at home. One young boy, Jan remembers, would spread his jacket on the floor and invite Baker to relax on it. Then, as with one hand he petted his companion, he read or tackled home work.

What about that mousing business which was to provide a role understood by all as a legitimate reason for having cats in the library? I suspect the first mice to come close enough to get a whiff of Baker and Taylor scampered off to pass the word around and all went looking for a safer refuge. Or perhaps there's not enough left of the alfalfa field to sustain many mice even through the summer. At any rate, the two cats, Baker and Taylor, are now entrepreneurs who need not stoop to posing as "Mouse patrol;" nor do they need to worry about the continuing good will of the library board.

We often say, "I smell a rat!" when, intuitively, we sense something is not quite right. Cats and mice use intuition too; although smell, in their case, may be an important element.

A friend recalled his days as a farm boy. At the time they had no cat, but did have a problem with mice. A neighboring farmer was asked to donate one of his cats. (Unless distemper had hit recently, farmers usually had a few to spare) The cat settled into his new home and within a week the mice all but disappeared. No cat could have killed all those mice in that length of time. The puzzle was solved when another neighbor, also without cats, mentioned how amazed he had been at the number of

One young boy spreads his jacket
on the floor and invites Baker
to lie down on it.

mice which appeared, almost overnight, at his farm. "Get a cat, as we did," he was told. "Until last week those mice were on our farm."

Verle Parker, librarian at the Aquatic Research Institute in Hayward, California also tells of how cats and mice reacted to each others presence at the research center. Institute cats, Jennie, Cream Puff, and Jane, were assigned the task of eradicating a population of field mice whose territory had been taken over by the Institute. These three cats, having been part of that library staff from early kittenhood, had absolutely no experience preparing them for undertaking this new assignment. Verle maintains, "Some innate instinct, some atavistic twinge startled them into taking an interest in the mouse or mice and the mice, being even more instinctual, took their approach as a severe warning." The mice disappeared. Assignment completed.

Now the Institute cats are free to concentrate on library procedures. Verle notes, "They have such a grave interest, turning their heads here and there to keep track of my every movement as if they thoroughly enjoy keeping abreast of the work I am doing. Often there is one on my desk staring with perseverance into my face as I check serials, type, or file; and if I move to another area I am sure to have company following in marching order as they come down the aisle, plop on the floor and make themselves comfortable. They often wash up in public on top of the highest shelves, discreetly (or indiscreetly) washing every part with an eye on things below. Our library would be a lonesome place without them — books and cats are great companions!"

Before Jennie, Cream Puff, and Jane there was Polar Bear. She too came to the Institute Library as a kitten, a

"Our library would be a lonely place without them. Books and cats make great companions".

foundling. Verle tells how Polar Bear learned to swing across the bars that held the bookshelves. "She resembled a little white monkey with golden eyes. And as to the mice, she did not alleviate the problem — she adopted them." So much for instinct.

Cats often do get established in libraries because of their traditional role as mousers. But sometimes they just drop in and personality takes it from there. Or, as in the case of "Dewey Readmore Books" they *get* dropped in. While still a very young kitten, Dewey came bouncing in through the book drop at the Public Library in Spencer, Iowa. He could hardly claim to have been sent to handle any mouse problems they might have. Since charm is a commodity in good supply when you're a cuddly kitten, this one had little trouble establishing himself.

A contest, participated in by library patrons, resulted in the selection of the name "Dewey Readmore Books." With a moniker like that he was destined to live out his life as a Library Cat. According to Vicki Myron, who admits to some prejudice, he has a loyal band of followers consisting of the staff plus anyone who stops in to check out a book. "I'm his Mom," Vicki declares as she totes him around the library on her shoulder.

Dewey has an impressive publicity record: First he appeared in the *Library Cat Newsletter*, then the magazine, *Country*. After that he became quite a celebrity with articles in *Cat Fancy* and *Wilson Library Bulletin* as well as other magazines and newspapers. Local television stations also scheduled interviews. But posing for pictures and being interviewed hasn't impressed Dewey. He just continues being his charming self as he rides on office chairs or wire book carts where feet and tail dangle

"I'm his mom," Vicki declares as she totes him around on her shoulder.

through the wires as he is happily transported to wherever library business takes him.

Dewey's life as Library Cat started the day he was wedged in among books in the book drop. This was an unpleasantly battering experience. Yet from that day books, patrons, and staff have been Dewey's life and love. "He likes ladders." adds Vicki. "If you get out one of the roller ladders, Dewey is right on it."

Sophie is another cat who "dropped in." Her drop was pretty impressive and, I might add, life threatening. Nor did she come alone, but with four kittens. But to start at the beginning:

The Walker Branch Library in Minneapolis is underground and located in what is known as "Uptown" where Hennepin Avenue and Lake Street intersect. It's a busy place with two theaters plus restaurants and shops of every kind. Young rebels with hair dyed green and men and women in business suits carrying briefcases pass each other without a second look. A thriving Uptown achieves its identity in this community of diversity.

In order to enter the library space, surrounded by a waist high wall, one must walk down several flights of stairs. On either side of the stairs are landscaped terraces with grass, flowers and trees. Finally you arrive at the cement landing which leads into the library.

It was on an evening in early summer that a patron, leaving the library, was startled to see a bag plummeting down to land on one of the terraces. For some moments there was no motion in the bag; then slowly and tentatively there emerged a small black and white cat. Behind her, four mewling kittens tumbled out. The startled patron hurried back inside to describe what she had seen.

The Humane Society could have been called. Or a

policeman in the area could have been handed the job of bringing the little family to the pound. Neither was done. Instead staff went home hoping that by morning the problem would have solved itself.

No such luck. Cat and kittens seemed to have decided that this was home. The appealing black and white cat was provided with food. Staff speculated about the person whose arm had dropped the bag. Fortunately, or maybe with forethought, the bag had been aimed straight down on to a surface softened by summer rains. Had the arm swung out in a curve the cats might have splattered on the hard, unforgiving pavement. Since the cats were not afraid of people, they apparently had not been previously mistreated. What pressures and desperation might have been behind this throw will never be known.

The Minneapolis Library Board was way ahead on anticipating this situation. They had spelled out quite clearly that there would be no pets in any of the city libraries. Nothing had been said about library grounds. An ad hoc adoption agency was established and library patrons were carefully interviewed as they applied to become the owners of "very special" kittens.

All was peaceful, if a bit worrisome for the future of the mother cat, until staff noticed that, just about the time they had placed the last kitten, their little feline was getting pretty big around the middle. Although they never saw or heard any other cat on the terraces, there must have been romancing going on at night. Their young tenant was well into her second pregnancy.

Some rules, even Library Board rules, are meant to be broken or at least suspended when humaneness

Cat and Kittens seemed to have decided,
for the time being, this was home.

demands it. Kitty couldn't have her second litter of kittens in a public, unsheltered place.

At about this time the last barrier to total acceptance was overcome and she was no longer just "the cat." Sophie became her name. She spent more and more time in the library workroom. Some cats in this illegal shelter would have blown the whole thing with their loud meowing. Not Sophie, she was a completely silent cat. And, although vibrations in her throat indicated purring, not even her purring was vocalized.

Sophie's second litter of four kittens (with good vocal cords) were born in a box in the knee-hole area under the supervising librarian's desk. Again the ad hoc adoption agency had work to do. All kittens were put up for adoption when they were old enough to climb out of the box to begin exploring. I believe these kittens hold the distinction of being the only associate LCS cats actually born in a library.

Pirate was one of the second litter of kittens and, like his mother, is black and white and, although he is not voiceless, he has a silent purr. It was reported by his present owners that he has " a calm and loving temperament and has turned into a hunter who has rid the household of mice." It is also reported that his favorite pastime, after hunting, is to curl up in the lap of anyone who is reading a good book. Early environment does make a difference! But where did he get his start as a hunter?

Sophie now lives a life of pampered luxury in the home of the Walker Library head librarian and is reported to be a most beautiful, intelligent, and special cat (spayed, of course) Walker Branch Library has, for some time, been completely law-abiding with no need of a functioning ad hoc adoption agency.

A five dollar fee will make you a member of the Library Cat Society and give you a one year subscription to the Newsletter. Send subscription request to: Phyllis Lahti, Editor, POB 274, Moorhead, Mn. 56560

Margaret, Fanny and Others

6. A Second Hand Bookstore
with Heart

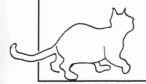

A Second Hand Bookstore
with Heart

"Cats in bookstores," Phyllis Lahti recalls, "once seemed more numerous and more visible than cats in libraries. Now the bookstore cat may be fast disappearing, along with its owner-operators, replaced by well-lighted book chains that do not have the kind of private spaces, the mysterious nooks and dark crannies, cats need for an occasional retreat."

Second hand bookstores, however, are flourishing, and the chances are good that you will find snuggled into one of those "mysterious nooks or crannies" a resident cat. An article in a St.Paul, Minnesota paper about a second hand bookstore called "Booksellers et al" included a picture of Fanny, the white and black cat who is considered a member of the staff. I decided on a visit.

Steve Anderson, a co-owner, was on duty. He said the person to talk to was Ruth Harper McKee, one of the partners in the business. "She is the cat person. But I can tell you about Fanny and how she happens to be here. On a below zero December day, a man had seen her, a starving, bedraggled kitten on a busy street. He picked her up and carried her into another book store a few blocks from here. There the manager refused to get involved in the rescue effort, saying, 'No way! But try the new store, Bookseller et al. I know they have one cat already.' (As all cat owners know, if you have one or more cats, everyone assumes you will surely want more)

"He was right in assuming that we couldn't refuse to give the kitten a home. Ruth works Fridays and Saturdays," Steve concluded. "Come back when she's on duty. She will be glad to talk to you."

I arranged a Friday morning interview with Ruth. The day I walked into Booksellers et al it was raining hard. I, who hate umbrellas and will usually insist I can run between the rain drops, was carrying one. Ruth met me at the door and suggested I leave the umbrella open and propped on the floor to dry. Thanking her, I arranged the dripping umbrella and looked around for Fanny, their Christmas cat.

The Fanny I saw relaxing in the front window was a far cry from that miserable little homeless cat who came through the door in the arms of a stranger that cold December day. She opened sleepy green eyes to look at her latest admirer and to greet me with her small meow. She stretched, yawned and, after studying my umbrella, decided it looked like a nice shelter under which to continue her nap.

More than likely Fanny's dreams are untroubled by memories of those early days on the city street. In fact, she is, I was told, a singularly untroubled cat. When there is no convenient umbrella available, and no kids are in sight, she simply stretches herself out on the floor of the central isle and fully expects that customers will side step her.

When awake Fanny tends to her duty as hostess and meets customers at the door. Ruth looked at their somewhat overweight cat with chagrin. "Her mind never wanders far from the thought of food. She sometimes

Attending to her duties, Fanny greets customers.

meets customers meowing hopefully, 'A small morsel for a starving cat?' One customer always carries a brief-case. Out of it, carefully wrapped, comes that treat for Fanny, a small piece of boiled liver or chicken. Nor will Fanny scorn a pinch of your morning doughnut. Some bring fresh catnip which Fanny finds great for rolling in as well as for nibbling. Customers who have forgotten the name of the store usually remember Fanny's name."

One shopper, allergic to cats, times his stay. He gives himself ten minutes, after which he asks for a box of tis-sues and quickly winds up his search for the right books.

While I was checking out the book shelves at the back of the store in the hope of finding some information about Ernest Hemingway's many cats, I heard a strange foghorn like sound, repeated at intervals. Curious as to the origin of that unexpected intrusion, I looked toward the entrance. A big dog, held on a leash by a man with a dripping umbrella in his other hand, repeated the sound. The dog was many times Fanny's size, yet he resembled her in being a bit overweight and being mostly white with some black spots. That foghorn sound was his ver-sion of barking.

Nobody seemed perturbed by the four footed visitor, not even Fanny. She looked casually in the dog's direc-tion, probably wishing kids who come in were no more threatening than the leashed dog. Fast moving children, Ruth said, send Fanny into rapid retreat behind the desk where she tucks herself in next to the paper book bags. Or, if the child is not too aggressive, she might escape by jumping up on the chair behind the counter, which is made comfortable with a bed pillow in a case patterned with white daisies and green leaves.

Sitting on Fanny's chair, I sipped hot coffee as Ruth

told of the many animals in her life. Fanny liked the sound of our voices and came to stretch out between us.

Fanny is not this store's first cat. Ready and waiting that hot summer in 1983 when Booksellers et al opened its doors for the first time was Margaret, a calico. She was homeless and hungry, but she hadn't given up on asking for help. People were emptying trucks and carrying in books. She meowed her insistence that they pay attention to her, that she needed someone to help her survive in this concrete jungle.

Ruth looked at the little intruder, who kept getting in her way as she hurried in and out making last minute arrangements, and knew only one thing to do. That cat needed food and water. Soon she understood that what the little calico was asking for was more. Kitty wanted to move in permanently.

The store space is large, and so is Ruth's heart. The little calico was invited to stay. She really took hardly any space at all. First she drank some water and gobbled a piece of Ruth's lunch. Then she sniffed her way through the store, rubbed her nose over surfaces to add her own scent to that of all the people who had passed that way. Finally it was time to curl her tired body into a quiet corner and close her eyes in sleep. She was already beginning to feel safe. Since that day she never asked to leave the store. Margaret knew a good thing when she found it.

For years Margaret had her own chair near the window where the winter sun could warm her and where she could watch both the activity on the street and in the store. At times, when she came to claim her chair, a customer was sitting there. Not even Fanny made this mistake. A calendar picture of a calico cat, with markings similar to Margaret, was located. Ruth cut this out and fastened it to the back of the chair. Above this was lettered, "Margaret's chair." Thus the chair was permanently reserved for one calico cat.

Since no one knows how old Margaret was when she joined the staff, Ruth can only guess that she may have been about 17 or 18 when kidney failure ended her reign at Booksellers et al.

Fanny, who arrived only six months after Margaret, was now alone and enjoyed getting all the attention. During the many "overlap" years, sales at the bookstore were featured as "Margaret and Fanny sales." Although this well organized store supplies many needs better than the large spit and polish chain store, the sales also drew those who came as much to see the two felines as to buy. Serious researchers and friendly visitors alike anticipate a relaxed and friendly atmosphere.

Ruth specializes in books on religion and theology. Steve knows the history books, and Ann, Ruth's daughter, will help readers wanting books on Hollywood, film, and cinema. Since second hand bookstores do not provide a lucrative income, everyone works at some other job as well. During her off hours Ruth offers genealogical research services.

"Animals have always been a part of my life," Ruth continued. "My mother was a cat lover. My father loved dogs. That's how our life ran. Mother was this, Dad was that, right down to party affiliations. Mother would bring home the stray kittens, and Father would find the dogs. I ended up loving both.

"I remember Tom and Jerry, cats who belonged to a bachelor relative. They grew and grew until they were each all of fifteen pounds of bone and muscle. I never did have a chance to pet them because the minute I entered the house they streaked for the basement." But wild they were not. Toward their owner they were trusting and loving. He accustomed them to the use of a harness and took them for daily walks on a leash. This was at a time when most cats roamed freely.

Ruth has since wondered about their origins. They had beautiful, semi-long, thick coats and long, luxurious tails. "Could their ancestors have interbred with the Bobcat?" This is not likely. It is possible to cross domestic cats with all kinds of wild cats, but the progeny are fragile and delicate, often die young, and rarely succeed in producing a second cross-breed generation.

Conversation turned to the Maine Coon Cat. We agreed that Tom and Jerry might well have been related to that sturdy cat. This brought up the question of its origins. In spite of the name, which implies that house cats and raccoons may interbreed, it's generally agreed this is genetically impossible. Some believe this big, handsome cat is a descendant of pets of sailors whose ships were wrecked on the rocky Maine coast. While others say kittens born during a voyage were left behind when after a stop the ship continued on its way.

To expand a bit on this idea, I shared another conjecture. These sailors may have come from Norway, and the cats sailing with them, destined to be the ancestors of the Maine Coon Cat, were Norway's "Skogkatter," (Forest Cats) who have wandered Norway's forests for centuries. Since trolls were said to inhabit the same deep forests and mountains, the cats were sometimes known as "troll cats."

Natural selection in a harsh climate weeds out all but those most suited to that environment. They need heavy, warm coats. They need to be good hunters, and intelligent enough to survive hazards of the forest. A Forest Cat, shipwrecked or abandoned on the Maine coast, would stand a good chance of survival in a severe climate.

My conclusion was that the Maine Coon Cat may have descended from Norway's Forest Cat, known in our country as a "Wegie." Possibly Tom and Jerry were such cats. Ruth agreed that this provided an interesting genealogical basis for her relative's big cats.

A customer, who had selected a number of books, claimed Ruth's attention. After the sale, Ruth joined me again and continued, "Many cats have shared my home. When one has left another has come to weave an unbroken chain. At present there is Mitten, a black cat with white paws, who stops whatever she is doing the minute I say her name. And there is Sweet Charity now 17 who spends most of her time sleeping. Daughter Ari named her.

"And we have dogs. Mamie is part Hound Dog. She arrived, as a little puppy, via a drop over my back yard fence. I had come home late. I was tired and preparing for early bedtime when I heard this racket in my yard. I opened the back door to investigate. There sat a puppy crying for someone to care for her. That evening, peace was a priority. I stepped out, picked up the little dog and snuggled her. She immediately stopped whining. I checked her carefully for fleas, then took her to my bedroom and dropped her onto my bed." Ruth laughed as she remembered "The puppy turned over on her back and, legs akimbo, closed her eyes and slept peacefully until morning." A brief visit to the back yard took care of toilet needs. The children looked at the new puppy and asked, "What do we do with her?"

Ruth answered without hesitation, "We're bonded. She's staying with us."

Then there's Lucky, a Border Collie. Abused by his former owners, he had never learned to socialize. Unlike most dogs, Lucky couldn't have cared less what people thought of his behavior. "I don't know how we would ever have reformed Lucky without the help of our Katie, who is part Poodle and part Lab. She took on the job of teaching the nervous, mistrusting Lucky how to behave. Although Lucky hasn't changed completely, Katie has worked wonders."

I asked Ruth, "Is there one cat who is most memorable?"

There was no hesitation. "That would be Bitsy. Two neighbor boys were playing ball with this long haired grey and white kitten. I saw the little body flying through the air. Sometimes they caught her and sometimes she hit the ground. I hurried over and caught the little animal on one throw as she came hurtling through the air."

"Hey that's our cat", one of the boys shouted. Ruth answered that they could have the cat back when one of the parents came and promised the cat would be cared for. No parent came. Only an older brother appeared to demand the cat's return. Bitsy remained with Ruth.

"Within a few days Bitsy had her first epileptic seizure. These continued at frequent intervals until a veterinarian prescribed medication which reduced the number and severity. But sometimes she didn't swallow the pill. Then, when the seizure hit, she became a whirling dervish. We quickly gathered any pillows readily at hand to cushion the blows she inflicted on herself as she hit hard objects near her.

"Bitsy had no depth perception. When she left a chair, she simply stepped off with no realization that she would drop a foot or more. She never took normal steps. She slid from place to place without lifting her feet. Her body was either completely rigid or completely relaxed. Occasionally she would stand up on her hind legs unable to get those front legs back on the floor. Eventually, unless someone came to her rescue, her rigid body tipped over backwards. When she was out in the yard, she moved slowly and hesitantly across the grass. If the lawn sprinkler was on and she came within reach of the spray she froze. What to do about this situation was beyond her."

"How did she handle the litter box?" I wondered.

Ruth laughed, "Oh, that was her nemesis. We spread papers around the box, because she often didn't quite make it into the litter. I think she might have been a little afraid of the texture. But we never scolded her. She tried so hard to please!

"Bitsy seemed incapable of anger, rebellion, resentment, or of making decisions for herself. Whatever triggers expressions of these reactions in a cat was lacking in Bitsy. She loved having her long hair combed. In fact, she loved any attention given her."

In order to keep Bitsy from being under foot, Ruth sometimes picked her up and carried the completely relaxed body on her arm. There she snuggled for as long as Ruth would hold her. Shortly after Bitsy's arrival, one of Ruth's daughters became subject to epileptic seizures. It was important to the family to teach children and adults about seizures and its effects. Bitsy became a part of these lessons. "We visited elementary schools and, with Bitsy's help, I think we did a good job of helping the children learn, not only about epilepsy, but about compassion and understanding."

Bitsy lived a short life. At age four she suffered from pressure behind her eyes, perhaps a tumor, the vet surmised. She deteriorated rapidly and it became necessary to end the life of the little cat who had so many problems, but who knew how to give love and was loved in return.

The morning had somehow vanished into noon. It was time to close my notebook, put away my pencil, and thank Ruth for so generously sharing time and memories of animals she had helped who had enriched her life in return,.

The rain had stopped and bright sunlight tumbled off the street and into the store. I could close my umbrella and return home to organize my information about Ruth, her bookstore, and her animals.

A Boarding Home for Felines

7. Madam Meadow's Cat House

Madam Meadow's Cat House

Madam Meadow's Cat House? Well, yes and no. It's perfectly legal. Those who come to use the facilities offered by the house are all four legged felines. And Alice Meadow is not really a "madam", but she finds the double meaning amusing. While working with her lawyer on the legal aspects of boarding cats, she spent a lot of time on the phone. When she was pretty sure the incoming call was from him, she sometimes answered the phone with the greeting, "Madam Meadow's Cat House." She remembers the long pause at the other end of the line as her lawyer tried to decide what his response should be. When I called to arrange a visit and to get instructions for driving to "Just Cats" she concluded her directions with, "When you arrive, knock three times and ask for Jo."

I wondered about her background. How did it happen that she chose a cat boarding facility as a business?

"During college years I was interested in everything in the field of liberal arts," Alice recalled. "This encompasses a wide range so I was well on the way to becoming a professional student before I left the campus for a career in advertising."

During these years she already had her two cats, Smudge and Orca. When travel took her from home, she left them with a woman who owned a boarding place for cats. When she heard that the business was up for sale, her thoughts turned to that empty building on her property. The structure had been used by a previous owner as a machine repair shop. Alice likes cats and enjoys contacts with people. Here was a chance to establish her own business. She decided to make an offer. Thus began the Alice Meadow cattery known as "Just Cats."

The day I visited the little red building, surrounded by trees and wild flowers, seventeen cats were vacationing there. Each had arrived with a supply of favorite food and perhaps a favorite toy as well. During the recent fourth of July week-end she catered to 28. That was a full house. The number of accommodations will most likely remain small, a size she can handle herself. The city of Minnetonka requires a special permit before allowing a business which employs help to locate in a residential area.

Alice and her cat Smudge (Smudge, and Orca live in "the big house") greeted us at the door to the cattery. Although Smudge does not lay claim to any distinguished heritage, in years past his charcoal grey coloring would probably have gained him the distinction of being called a Maltese. Or perhaps there was a Russian Blue in his ancestry. When Alice acquired Smudge he was a very different looking cat. Instead of his solid charcoal grey color and green eyes, he had violet eyes, white tipped grey fur, and burgundy nose and pads. Alice declared, as she picked him up to give him a hug, "Everything changed except his loving personality. He's a cuddler!"

"Most unusual," I mused. I was almost ready to ask if she was certain Smudge had not been kidnapped by some trouble making trolls. Perhaps this was not really

Smudge, but a "changeling" left in his place. Norse folk lore tells of trolls who played such tricks on their human neighbors. Later I decided to inquire of several authorities on cats about color changes. I was told by one that such changes, as a cat matures, are not unusual. I'm still not completely dismissing that troll connection.

Both Orca and Smudge came from the local Humane Society. Orca was busy elsewhere and did not greet us. "His coloring is black and white," Alice explained, "so I call him 'Orca' which is the scientific name for the Killer Whale, who is also black and white in much the same pattern." There ends the resemblance.

At first Orca and Smudge were not pleased with all those visiting cats. It seemed their territory had been invaded by an army of strangers. They stayed as far away from the building as possible. They're now used to it all and pay little attention to the occupants of the little red building. Smudge did opt to stay outside as Alice invited us in to the office area. At one end of the room is a desk with a telephone, an answering machine, and a radio on which Alice often tunes in classical music for herself and the cats. A large window above the desk frames the wooded outdoor scene. At the opposite end of the rectangular space is a storage room for supplies. Here is kept, carefully labeled, that special food which comes with each cat.

Centrally located on the north wall is a screened door leading from the office area into the boarding apace. This large room, occupying the remainder of the building, is painted a delicate peach-cream. The medium grey "apartments" are spacious and well equipped. Alice explained that although cats are believed not to have our color perception (where we see primary colors, they see

All the apartments have three levels

pastels) Color emits vibrations for them, as for us, and subdued, soothing colors are important. White towels lined each bed. Light green and white print curtains served as partitions for privacy. Name tags were fastened to each unit with colored clothes pins. Alice knew all 17 cats by name and introduced us to the five whose apartment doors had been left open. All were using the opportunity to wander about the room. Two cats did disturb the peace with a brief hissing encounter, causing one to hurriedly retreat to the safety of an open compartment. "Not his compartment," Alice laughed. But it seemed to provide the security he needed.

Alice has permitted (while she is there to insure the peace) as many as 20 cats the freedom of the room at the same time. But she is more likely to rotate, allowing no more than five out at any one time. None has been there long enough to consider this personal territory. Also, all cats accepted for boarding care have been neutered, thus decreasing territorial behavior. "This is neutral ground," Alice explained. It occurred to me that they might also recognize that starting a fight with that number around would be dangerous business.

Alice remembers one exception to this non-aggressive behavior. Harry's owner spent the winter in the Southwest. Since Harry didn't enjoy all that traveling, it was arranged that he would stay the winter with Alice. He eventually decided this busy place, with cats coming and going, was home and took to defending his territory, making it more difficult to give the short term occupants the freedom they needed.

All the apartments have three levels. The first level contains the litter trays, which are cleaned daily. The food dishes, sterilized daily, are also on the lower level but placed a distance away from the enclosed and out-of-sight litter pans. (Some cats object to having their food near the toilets) Beds, circular,and padded, are on the second level. The third and uppermost area could be considered the parlor. It's just for relaxing and for viewing neighbors.

One group of four apartments can be opened up to make a "condo" in case someone brings in two, three, or four cats who will feel more comfortable if they are able to move freely, via carpeted ramps, to visit one another.

Floors are not constructed of wire, as is often the case in boarding places, but of painted wood. If a cat seems more secure in a small area, he is given one of the smaller quarters. One apartment was completely enclosed by curtains to give the nervous occupant a chance to settle down and possibly to keep him from disturbing others by his loud meowing. One boarder refused to eat until the lower part of of his space was encircled by cloth.

Alice knows that boarding in her facility is not like home, but she uses every means at her disposal to make her guests happy and comfortable. A ceiling fan circulates the air and, in the winter, a heating unit keeps the building warm. A "monkey tree" in the commons area, reaching from floor to ceiling, invites the climbers to exercise. Although most of the cats who come are declawed, all like to go through the motions of "sharpening" their claws. Also, of course, they still have claws on their hind feet which help them to climb. At the foot of the tree is an assortment of toys inviting to play time.

Pure-bred cats are more high strung and take longer to adjust. A Siamese was quietly pacing his quarters. He had not been there long and was still unhappy with the placement. A small Abyssinian loudly announced that he did not like this arrangement. Later in the day each would get his turn to wander through the room. Perhaps they would then be happier.

William, a beautiful all white cat, with one green eye and one blue eye, was sitting quiet and relaxed in his compartment. As is so often true of white cats with blue eyes (or one blue eye) he is totally deaf. Having never heard himself meow, he has no way of knowing how to adjust his meowing to suit the occasion. Alice said, "Instead of meowing, he screams."

All the cats want attention and petting. Alice obliges although sometimes she gets scratched or bitten for her efforts. She explained it this way, "They suffer from attention deficit. They want and need petting but some-times get angry because I'm not the right person. They miss their familiar people."

Alice told about a local family, consisting of husband, wife, and five cats, who were in the throes of relocating to the West coast. The wife had already moved to Seattle where she was hoping to find a suitable residence.

The husband, back in Minnesota, was trying to sell their house. It was a slow business. The real estate agent thought perhaps people might be turned off by the sight of five cats roaming through the house and suggested boarding them. They were all brought to the cattery. Four adjusted fairly well, but Major meowed loudly and constantly. Since these were summer days with mellow weather, Alice placed Major in a large cage, carried him out and set the cage on a broad tree stump. All around him were tall grasses and trees. Major stopped meowing and spent his time enjoying the wonderful world of trees, flowers, birds, and fresh air. As long as he could remain in his tree house he was, Alice related, "relaxed and happy as a clam."

Eventually the Minneapolis home did sell and all five cats were shipped to Seattle where, since the new house was not yet available, they shared the home of a woman who agreed to take them in until things got settled.

Vincent, a Siamese, takes the prize for unusual behavior. When he was brought in for boarding, his owner left a man's heavy white cotton sock for his compartment. Alice assumed this was something with which he enjoyed playing, but she soon noted that each time he finished eating his canned food he went to the sock, placed one paw firmly at one end, then bit into the sock and allowed his teeth to slip the entire length. That he was effectively cleaning his teeth was clear when Alice examined the sock. Small particles of food had adhered the length of the area used. When Alice shared her amazement, the owner exclaimed, "I'm so glad you saw this. I've told the vet and he shakes his head and maintains it is coincidental."

If you search your area with care you may find similar accommodations which make it possible for you to have the delight of a cat or two and yet make plans to travel without worry. "Just Cats" and other facilities designed to provide for both basic and individual needs may not be your cat's first choice. A well cared for cat has a strong conviction that "There is no place like home." But it's reassuring to know that your cat will be well cared for and in good health when he returns home.

Coincidentally, just as I was collecting information about "Just Cats" I learned that half a continent and an ocean away Ingvald and Inga, in Ulrica, Sweden, have also decided to convert unused buildings on their land into boarding facilities for cats. I don't have all the details about their "Katt Pension" but they write that each space has a scratching post, small bed, and an easy chair. They even have rugs on the floor and pictures on the walls. Their commons area has a large window in front of which the cats can sun themselves as they relax or watch the outdoor scene. Inga declares that cat owners come from as far as twenty-five miles to leave their cats and that the cats have responded well to all the efforts on their behalf.

Perhaps, one day, someone will plan an international convention where Alice, Ingvald, Inga, and all the other entrepreneurs can meet with people of many countries to exchange ideas on how to better meet needs of people and animals through the use of small temporary residences.

"Mogs" of the British Museum

8. Guardians of Treasure

Guardians of Treasure

It seems that mice have a special affinity for libraries and museums and the English have a special affinity for cats and dogs. So perhaps it is not surprising to find that the British Museum, located on Bloomsbury Street in London since the middle of the 18th century, has a history of Museum cats as long as the history of the Museum itself.

Hans Sloane (1660-1753) the Irish doctor and one-time president of the Royal Society whose books, art, and natural history specimens were the foundation on which other Museum collections were built is said to have owned fifteen cats.

There is also documented proof that the Keeper of Manuscripts, Sir Frederic Madden, who was on the staff from 1828 to 1866, owned two cats. Both were imported from France and were allowed anywhere Sir Madden was found. One was named Mouton and had so endeared himself to Sir Frederic that when he died his body was turned over to a taxidermist to be stuffed and mounted so that his memory would better live on. When Sir Frederic's voluminous diary is published we will likely have available a great deal more about his two French cats.

Another cat with a recorded history is Black Jack. "In the early 1900's when Dr. Richard Garnett ruled over the Department of Printed Books, Black Jack, a handsome black creature with a white shirt-front, white paws and whiskers of great length, was a frequent visitor." It's not clear if he belonged to anyone in particular, or if he had just come in off the street and decided this was a good place to stay. He was fond of sitting on the desk in the magnificent blue-domed Reading Room where renowned writers and philosophers have scribbled and where students and tourists with the coveted reading card feel fortunate to spend the day. The room is said to "envelope the user with an un-British warmth." Perhaps that warmth was the special appeal which attracted Black Jack. He never hesitated to ask a reader to hold open the folding doors when he wanted in or out.

He very likely earned his right to the Reading Room by keeping mice in check and held a secure place until one Sunday when he got himself into serious trouble. Black Jack found himself locked into the newspaper room with no one to open the door. The day dragged on and he was getting bored. Looking around he decided the leather bindings on volumes of old newspapers were good material on which to sharpen his claws.

Monday morning when the Museum opened the keeper of the room was horrified by the amount of damage Black Jack had done to the leather bindings. Black Jack was in disgrace.

Not only was Black Jack banished from the library but the Clerk of the Works was ordered to get rid of him. The problem was that Black Jack had mysteriously disappeared. It was "whispered about" that two staff members were keeping him in hiding and providing him with food.

After a bit things settled down. The Clerk of the Works dutifully reported that the offending cat had dis-

They are part of the Museum staff. Law officers who guard against thieves who "break in and nibble."

appeared and was "presumed dead." The bindings of the volumes were repaired and "the official mind was once more at peace." A few weeks later Black Jack was back at his favorite place in the Reading Room. The chief officials asked no more questions.

Undoubtedly there were other cats on Museum "rat patrol" but they remain unrecorded in Museum history. Black Jack was top cat and when not sleeping in some sunny window he patrolled the grounds. On one such excursion Black Jack found Mike who lived to become the most recorded and longest living of British Museum cats.

It was the year 1908 when Black Jack was seen by the Keeper of Egyptian cat mummies carrying something in his mouth. He brought his burden to the Keeper and dropped it at his feet. After looking up into the man's face, he turned and walked away. That "burden" was later known to fame as "Mike." The Keeper of the mummies picked up the little creature and arranged to care for him. The Keeper's other two cats soon adopted Mike and helped in his upbringing.

Sir E. A. Wallis Budge, Keeper of Egyptian Antiquities, retired in 1924. He had many memories of the years Mike had been an amusing and relaxing part of his days. So when Mike died in 1929 at the age of 21, Sir Wallis decided to write the story of Mike's life as he remembered it and as it had been recorded when Mike had at various times broken into print.

Sir Wallis recalled that when Mike was old enough to do his own exploring he made friends with the gatekeeper at the main gate. He began to spend a great deal of time at the lodge which was the "on the grounds" home of the gatekeeper.

The cat already there accepted Mike and assumed the job of properly training him to assist in the stalking of pigeons in the colonnade. Sir Wallis remembers how one Sunday, when there were few visitors around, Mike took on the job of pointing like a dog while the other cat, little by little, drove the pigeons into a corner. " When the pigeons became dazed and fell down, each cat seized a bird and carried it into the house uninjured. The house-keeper took the pigeons from the cats and in exchange gave each cat a slice of mutton and milk. She then moved the pigeons into a little side room and, after they had eaten some maize and drunk water, they flew out of the window none the worse for their handling by the cats. The fact was neither cat liked to eat game with dirty, sooty feathers; they preferred clean, cooked meat."

Eventually Mike moved "bag and baggage to the lodge where he was given more freedom to be the cat he wanted to be." This included "proceedings during the hours of night."

A corner shelf out of the drafts was prepared for him to sleep on. From there he could go out or come in at any time he pleased both by day and by night. The Keeper of the Egyptian cat mummies still kept a watchful, paternal eye on Mike and took care that he was never short of food. During the war years even though food was rationed Mike always curled up to sleep with a full stomach. "Whoever went short, Mike did not."

Not only did the pigeons feel the presence of Mike; "He took great interest in all that went on in the court-yard and was especially useful in chivying out the strange dogs that wandered in from time to time. Dogs,

Mike at first limited himself to
"pointing" while the house cats
little by little drove the pige[ons]
into a corner.

100

who laughed at policemen and gatekeepers, fled in terror before the attack of Mike who, swelling himself to twice his normal size, hurled himself at them. On such occasions he was truly a 'savage beast'."

Mike limited his friendship to a few favored people and disliked the attention of Museum visitors. On hot afternoons keepers often closed the east gate and crossed to the west for shade. Mike followed, but he wasn't happy with the change because on the west side there was no quick escape from the attention of the tourists. On the east Southhampton side there is a ledge over the lodge door. Two leaps and he was safely out of reach. The hard granite of the perch was eventually worn smooth by the impact of his feet.

When the Keeper of Egyptian mummies retired Mike, also ready for retirement, was declared a pensioner. This assured him of food, care, lodging and love for the remainder of his life. Each time the ex-Keeper returned to visit friends he checked to see that Mike was properly cared for. And Mike seeing his old friend came eager to be picked up, stroked, talked to and perhaps treated to a special tidbit.

At age 21 Mike's health began to fail and arrangements were made to feed him with "tender meat and fish" alternately. But old age could not be cured. It was agreed that the "Cats' Home" would have to take over.

A memorial poem in his honor was written by F.C.W. Hiley. In one section he attributes Mike's long life to his knowing of that famed hound, Argus:

> "Of Argus, that famed hound of old
> Who lived through hunger, heat and cold;
> And when his lord came home at last,

101

> When twenty years were well-nigh past,
> Looked up, and wagged his tail and died.
> But Michael, stiff with feline pride,
> Vowed, by a dog he'd not be beat,
> And set himself to cap that feat."

In another part of the poem Hiley remembers Mike's anti-social behavior:

> "He cared for none save only two
> For these he purred, for these he played,
> And let himself be stroked, and laid
> Aside his anti-human grudge,"

However his longevity is explained, he did live to be a "pussy cat Methuselah." He was the most famous of Museum cats, but he was not the last.

Briefly mentioned in the Museum records is Belinda, a Ginger Tom, who is remembered for being a "strong character given to keeping warm on motor cars." He was succeeded by Suzie a black and white cat who" early abandoned the rough life of other strays and moved in with the warders." She never missed a patrol of the buildings. But when they arrived at the Sepulchral Basement she left, often to go back to the Colonnade to pounce on unsuspecting pigeons.

Unlike her predecessor Mike, Suzie liked people. She had a particular fondness for Jack Keilthy, one of the warders, and would wait for him to appear for duty.

Suzie lived to be 16 and on her death the British Museum Bulletin ran the following memorial:

"The Museum regrets having to announce the death of one of its long-serving members of staff. Suzie, the

Mike lived to be a "pussy-cat Methuselah".

black and white cat familiar to generations of visitor and staff, died at the age of 16 on May 20, 1982."

In the early days of Suzie's reign it appears there were more strays or "mogs," as they are called, than could be handled. When disposing of them was under consideration Maisie Webb, Deputy Director, became involved in helping to establish The Cats' Protection Society. With the assistance of other such organizations, they were able to catch, neuter, and find homes for those found on the Museum grounds.

Six, including Suzie, were kept. This has continued to be the number legally allowed on the grounds.

A letter from the Royal Society for the Prevention of Cruelty to Animals on file at the Museum states: "To retain a small colony of neutered feral cats whose general welfare is safeguarded by a corps of volunteers, is an extremely proficient and effective method of controlling an undesirable rodent insurgence."

Although cats had always been on Museum grounds, rules and guidelines were now established. Rex Shepherd, a member of the Museum's work staff, and chairman of the Cats' Welfare Society, has looked after the cats for the last 15 years. The Society publishes a newsletter and arranges for the annual Cats' Christmas Dinner collection. It was Rex who rescued Maisie and her brood from under a builder's hut and arranged for them to live on (or take over) the Museum grounds.

Mario who cleans the forecourt has made friends with Maisie and her offspring, Pippin, Poppet, and Pinkie and can probably tell you where they are at almost any time of the day. Maisie usually keeps Mario company as

Pippin stalking across the colonnade just as royalty approached.

he goes about his work in the early morning before the Museum opens to the public.

Ms. Caygill in the Museum Director's office tells of an evening visit by the Princess of Wales when they were concerned to see Pippin stalking across the colonnade through the welcoming delegation just as the Princess's car approached. Pippin had probably heard the old expression, "A tuppeny cat may look at a king though His Majesty pays no regard."

One visitor remembers seeing a black cat with an elegant white mask ascending a wide stone staircase "for all the world like some duchess going to a ball." A guard said this was Suzie the Second. Until recently Suzie the Second also spent a great deal of time in the Control Room. Visiting workmen who did not mind their manners were sometimes severally reprimanded by a swift and sharp bite. Perhaps this helped them to sympathize with the fate which befell errant mice who happened within reach of Suzie the Second's teeth. Eventually Rex decided Suzie was growing too old for life in the Control Room and retired her to a private home where her life would be less demanding.

Since 1972 the Library has been a separate entity and is now in the process of removing itself physically with the aim of having as much as possible of the voluminous collection of books and manuscripts on one site.

One "mog" has been seen at the site of the excavation. He seems to be waiting to move in. Perhaps there will be job openings there for six more "guardians of treasure." They're likely already lining up to make applications.

We're in Good Company
A Fantasy
9. When the Cat Got
My Tongue

When the Cat Got My Tongue

With the exception of a few acknowledged flights into fantasy or conjecture, I have not strayed from factual accounts in the stories you have already read. I am about to do a complete turn around by inviting you to come with me into a twilight world or as story tellers used to say into never,never land. If this gives you pause, perhaps the world of dreams will suit you better. So, we begin a journey:

We're dressed and ready for a dinner party. We don't know who else will be there nor where the dinner will be held. The message, which appeared as on a screen last evening while we sat relaxed after a day's work, simply read: "Dress for dinner tomorrow. You will be dining with important people from times past. When ready be seated and wait."

Suddenly we are at our destination. It must have taken a bit long to get "ready" because we have arrived late. The other guests are seated at the dinner table. To my astonishment I recognize Winston Churchill. Never mind that he has been dead for many years. So have the other guests. We, the late ones, are the exception.

On Churchill's right sits a petite, round faced woman with delicate features which are wreathed in a warm smile. Her rather large name plate assures me that, yes, this is Rachel Carson. When I look to Churchill's left and see my name I have a feeling of panic which accelerates as I make my way to my assigned place where Ernest Hemingway is seated to my left.

Whatever shall I find to say to these famous people? I'm almost paralyzed but I manage to sit down. I don't recognize the other guests. I'm too far away to read the name plates. Their haircuts and their clothing confirm that they too have been missing from the land of the living for some time before coming together for a memorial feast .

Conversation buzzes around me. I sit mute and embarrassed. What do I have in common with the three nearest me? I would make a fool of myself if I tried to talk to Churchill about English politics or World War Two. I remember that he liked to paint landscapes for relaxation. But what do I know about landscape painting? I could mention that I have visited Chartwell, the place they say Churchill liked best in all the world. As I recall my visit there one summer's day I remember Tango the beautiful tangerine cat who was also wandering around the estate. Perhaps Churchill has lost touch with Chartwell and hasn't heard that when Tango the first died a search was initiated to find a cat as much like Tango as possible to take his place. I'm not sure if the Tango I saw is the third or perhaps the fourth cat to carry on the tradition.

Churchill loved his cat and allowed him all kinds of outrageous privileges. If I could get him started talking about Tango and other animals on the estate, conversation would be no problem. Perhaps he would tell how he enjoyed walking the estate in the morning, even including a visit to the pig sty. In one account he was quoted as saying, "I like pigs. Cats look down on human beings, dogs look up to them, but pigs just treat us as their equals." I could remind him of that and we would enjoy a good laugh together. I'm beginning to thaw.

I sneak a look to my left. Whatever can I say to the great Hemingway? I could try to talk about his writing. Yet, I feel a little awkward about that. And if he brings up the subject of bull fighting or big game hunting, I might either remain mute or become obnoxiously negative. He did have a dog he was very fond of, and I know many pampered cats ran freely in his Key West home.

As I sneak a second look toward Hemingway a ginger cat with huge front paws takes shape in his arms. Hemingway is cupping one of the polydactyl paws in his hand as he explains to the person on his left about his seven toed cats. I reach out to stroke the cat's head, but he fades away and Hemingway is left sitting with empty arms, laughing as he explains, "That cat always was an independent cuss."

By now I'm relaxed enough to turn to Rachel Carson. Sincerely and enthusiastically I can tell her how much the world needed and still needs her book, SILENT SPRING. I may be uneasy if the subject turns to marine biology. She knows so much. I am overawed and afraid of asking silly questions. Then I remember, Paul Brooks biography, THE HOUSE OF LIFE, which mentions Rachel's devotion to cats. I can ask about her two Persions, Buzzie and Kito, and encourage her to tell again how Buzzie kept her company on her writing table as she worked late into the night to meet a deadline and how she relaxed from her work by pausing to sketch his little head drooping with sleepiness. Perhaps she will also tell of Muffin, a little grey kitten who came into her home when the Persians had ended their reign. Brooks quotes Carson as saying, "Muffin is now a full fledged associate who has travelled about 2000 miles with my mother and me."

By now I can look around me. My face is no longer fixed in a permanent smile which does not reach my eyes. I'm among friends. We can exchange stories all evening. When the evening closes and we return to the real world (or when the rest leave for the place they came from) there will still be tales that Hemingway, Churchill, Carson, and I didn't have time to tell.

I do not recall food being eaten. After all, only you and I have need of it. Instead the feast is one of stories, mostly animal stories. (Was this subject pre-ordained, or did you and I turn the conversation in that direction?) Cat people are the most vociferous and seemed to be using more than their share of the time. The whole table rings with good humor until suddenly the guests melt into shadows. Except for us the room is empty. In another instant we find ourselves alone in our easy chairs, back in our slippers and comfortable leisure clothing with only memories of a feast of stories.

The wonderful thing about this feast is that anyone and everyone who wishes can join me. Imagination and dreams allow for events not possible in the world of reality.